EARTH'S PRECIOUS
WATER
THE POWER OF WATER

by John Willis

LIGHTB◆X
openlightbox.com

LIGHTBOX

Go to
www.openlightbox.com,
and enter this book's
unique code.

ACCESS CODE

LBXQ2536

Lightbox is an all-inclusive digital solution for the
teaching and learning of curriculum topics in an original,
groundbreaking way. Lightbox is based on National
Curriculum Standards.

STANDARD FEATURES OF LIGHTBOX

AUDIO High-quality narration using text-to-speech system

ACTIVITIES Printable PDFs that can be emailed and graded

SLIDESHOWS Pictorial overviews of key concepts

VIDEOS Embedded high-definition video clips

WEBLINKS Curated links to external, child-safe resources

TRANSPARENCIES Step-by-step layering of maps, diagrams, charts, and timelines

INTERACTIVE MAPS Interactive maps and aerial satellite imagery

QUIZZES Ten multiple choice questions that are automatically graded and emailed for teacher assessment

KEY WORDS Matching key concepts to their definitions

Contents

The Natural Power of Water

Water is one of the most plentiful and important substances on Earth. However, people may take the power of water for granted. While water is an essential resource for sustaining plant and animal life, it is also involved in some of the most devastating natural disasters in recorded history.

Many kinds of natural disasters are water-related. Floods, avalanches, and mudslides can bury entire towns. Tropical storms and hurricanes, caused by changes in the weather, can flood vast areas of land. **Tsunamis**, which can be caused by the movement of Earth's **tectonic plates** or by landslides, may also result in flooding.

Natural disasters were named because they are typically caused by events that happen in nature, rather than by the actions of people or other **organisms**. However, this is not always the case. Today, human actions such as building **dams** or skiing may also cause disasters such as floods or avalanches to occur.

Since oceans and lakes allow for large amounts of goods to be moved by boat, people often live near bodies of water. In fact, 14 of the 15 largest cities on Earth are found near the coast. This is why natural disasters involving water may destroy property or harm people. While many natural disasters cannot be prevented, it is possible to design and build cities and towns in order to withstand them. Many types of natural disasters can also be **predicted**. This helps more people stay safe when they happen.

Mudslides have been recorded in **every U.S. state**.

The 2017 hurricane season was **the most expensive** in U.S. history.

In 1958, the **largest-known tsunami** took place in Alaska.

Tropical Cyclones

Hurricanes are the largest, most powerful storms on Earth. Depending on where it formed, a hurricane may be known as a typhoon instead. Both hurricanes and typhoons are also known as tropical cyclones. All hurricanes form above the warm waters near Earth's **equator**. Warm water heats the air above it. This warm air rises and is replaced by colder air from higher in the sky. This movement creates a cycle of spinning air above the water, forming what is known as a tropical depression.

When a tropical depression reaches wind speeds of 39 miles (63 kilometers) per hour, it is considered to be a tropical storm. If it reaches wind speeds of 74 miles (119 km) per hour, it is considered a hurricane or typhoon. Hurricanes keep growing in strength until they run out of warm water. This can happen when a hurricane pulls up cold water from the ocean depths. If a hurricane reaches land, it will also run out of warm water to use. However, a great deal of damage may occur before this happens.

Once a hurricane reaches the shore, it can cause a sudden rise in water levels. This is called a storm surge. In many cases, storm surges are the deadliest part of a hurricane. Hurricane winds are also very damaging. In strong hurricanes, these winds can tear down buildings and uproot trees. Tornadoes can also form inside of hurricanes. While most hurricanes have fewer than 10 tornadoes once they reach land, some have generated more than 140.

HURRICANE CATEGORIES

A hurricane's category is based on the strength of its wind. The category can be used to determine how dangerous a storm may be.

Category 1	**Wind Speed** 74–95 miles (119–153 km) per hour	**Minimum** Damage
Category 2	**Wind Speed** 96–110 miles (154–177 km) per hour	**Moderate** Damage
Category 3	**Wind Speed** 111–129 miles (178–208 km) per hour	**Extensive** Damage
Category 4	**Wind Speed** 130–156 miles (209–251 km) per hour	**Extreme** Damage
Category 5	**Wind Speed** Greater than 157 miles (252 km) per hour	**Catastrophic** Damage

Although 1.2 million people evacuated New Orleans, tens of thousands more were unable to leave.

Many local government organizations were flooded and unable to help people.

Hurricane Katrina was the costliest hurricane in U.S. history.

Hurricane Katrina

When: August 9, 2005 | **Where:** New Orleans, Louisiana

While New Orleans was not directly struck by Hurricane Katrina, much of the city is below sea level. Although New Orleans was protected by **levees** and drainage canals, the hurricane's storm surge overwhelmed them and flooded more than 80 percent of the city. It would take 43 days for this water to be drained. Hurricane Katrina caused more than $100 billion in damages. About 1,800 people were killed, and hundreds of thousands more lost their homes.

DISCUSSION
What steps might help prevent floods similar to those caused by Hurricane Katrina from happening again? Explain how these steps would be effective.

More than 60,000 people in New Orleans needed to be rescued from their rooftops.

Hurricane Katrina made landfall along the Gulf Coast of the United States.

More than 10,000 people sought shelter in the Louisiana Superdome.

Floods can happen in nearly any place on Earth. This includes arid locations, such as Nizwa, Oman.

Floods

A flood occurs any time a body of water rises beyond its normal banks and begins to cover dry land. There are many possible causes of floods. They can be created by other natural disasters, such as a hurricane's storm surge or a tsunami's impact on a coast. Other floods are seasonal. Some rivers flood regularly each year. When structures such as dams collapse, the sudden movement of water can also cause a flood.

Flash floods are among the most dangerous kinds of floods. They are some of the deadliest natural disasters in the United States. These floods occur when large amounts of snow melt, when there is torrential rain, or when a structure such as a dam or levee breaks. Flash floods are named because they happen so quickly. They can occur mere minutes after their triggering event. Flash floods are especially dangerous in towns or cities. The buildings and roads prevent water from being taken into the ground, causing water to stay on the surface without being absorbed.

Flash floods may uproot trees, move boulders, or cause mudslides. The fast-moving water and **debris** can cause people to lose their footing and drown. Water levels may rise by more than 30 feet (9 meters) during a flash flood. The worst flood in U.S. history took place when a dam broke in Johnstown, Pennsylvania, in 1889.

The seasonal flooding of the Nile River in Egypt allowed ancient Egyptians to have enough water to grow essential crops.

Since flash floods can happen very quickly, people can stay safe by keeping away from rivers or floodplains during or shortly after rain. In the United States, the National Weather Service (NWS) releases warnings to let people know if a flood is about to take place. The NWS has more than 100 field offices which are used to predict floods and storms.

The **Johnstown flood killed** more than 2,200 people.

The 1889 **dam break** caused **20 million tons** (18 million metric tons) of water to strike **Johnstown**.

The **Johnstown flood destroyed** the northern half of the city. More than **1,500 buildings** were **washed away**.

Tsunamis

The term *tsunami* is a Japanese word meaning "harbor wave." Tsunamis are formed when an earthquake or other **seismic** event takes place underwater. This creates a series of waves.

A tsunami wave slows to a speed of 20 to 30 miles (32 to 48 km) per hour when it reaches a shore.

Tsunami waves move quickly across the ocean. However, they are not very large at this time. When one of the waves approaches the shore, the seafloor begins to slow down the bottom part of the wave. The top part still moves quickly, though, causing the wave to rise up to greater heights. By the time a tsunami wave hits the shore, it can be more than 30 feet (9 m) tall.

The effect of a tsunami depends on where it hits the land and on the structure of the shore. Some coastal features, such as **coral reefs**, can make tsunamis smaller and less damaging. In some cases, tsunamis will pull water away from the shore before hitting land. This may make it appear as though the tide is going out.

2004 Indian Ocean Tsunami

The 2004 Indian Ocean Tsunami was caused by one of the strongest earthquakes on record. Since tsunamis in the area are so rare, there were no warning systems in place.

Death Toll: More than 225,000
Countries affected: 14

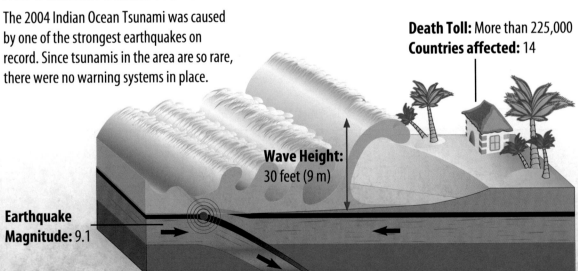

Wave Height: 30 feet (9 m)

Earthquake Magnitude: 9.1

A tsunami that struck Japan in 2011 destroyed about 120,000 buildings and damaged more than 1 million others.

Some tsunamis can raise water levels by as much as 100 feet (30 m) when they reach the shore. However, most tsunamis cause the water level to rise about 10 feet (3 m). This rise in water levels can cause flooding and put people at risk of drowning. These floods can reach more than 1,000 feet (300 m) onto land. When a tsunami hits the shore, the waves can uproot trees or destroy buildings.

More tsunamis are formed in the Pacific Ocean than anywhere else on Earth. However, they can occur in any ocean, such as the Indian Ocean Tsunami that occurred in 2004. The United States has two early warning centers in the Pacific. They are in Honolulu, Hawai'i, and Palmer, Alaska. These centers provide warnings to more than 26 different countries.

Avalanches

An avalanche occurs when a large amount of debris falls down the slope of a mountain. Although there are different kinds of avalanches, the most common are snow avalanches. They can happen any place where there are snow-covered mountains.

There are many causes of an avalanche. Heavy snowfall or falling trees and ice can cause an avalanche because of the extra weight. However, most of the avalanches that are dangerous to people are actually caused by humans. Many fatal avalanches occur due to skiers, snowboarders, and snowmobilers moving over weak points in snow.

On December 13, 1916, during World War I, about 200,000 tons (180,000 metric tons) of snow fell on a military base near Italy's Mount Marmolada. More than half of the 500 soldiers stationed there were killed.

Since many avalanches are caused by humans, there are steps that can be taken to prevent them from happening. Avalanche forecasters look at where avalanches have happened in the past, along with recent weather, in order to predict when and where future avalanches may occur. In areas where dangerous avalanches could happen, people may use explosives or cannons to start them when no one is around. In frequently-traveled areas, such as slopes alongside roads, people may build sets of fences to help support the snow and stop it from breaking into slabs.

Parts of an Avalanche

An avalanche occurs when there is a weak area in the snow on a slope. When something triggers this area, the snow will slide downhill. If the weak area is near the surface of the snow, it may make a sluff. A sluff is made of loose, powdery snow, and is not usually very dangerous. However, if a weak area is deeper in the snow, a slab avalanche may form. This can cause very large chunks of snow to break off and slide downhill. A slab avalanche can reach speeds of more than 80 miles (130 km) per hour.

An avalanche is made of three main parts.

1 Starting Zone

This is a weak area of snow on a slope. Although most starting zones are high on a slope, they can be found on any part of one.

2 Avalanche Track

This is the path the avalanche follows. In areas with frequent avalanches, it is often treeless.

3 Runout Zone

This is the flat area where the snow and debris come to a stop. Rescue workers will typically focus on the runout zone when searching for survivors.

Mudslides

A mudslide occurs when a piece of the ground turns to mud and moves downhill. Mudslides are caused when the ground becomes full of water, which is unable to drain. Often, this water is from heavy rains or melting snow. Construction, erosion, and the destruction of plants can all contribute to mudslides.

In 2017 and 2018, the state of California experienced several extreme weather events. In late 2017, large wildfires swept across the state. California also suffered from a major **drought** during the year. These two events may have contributed to the mudslides that took place shortly after.

Mudslides can be caused by other disasters. When Hurricane Maria struck Puerto Rico in 2017, the storm caused numerous floods and mudslides throughout the territory.

The drought that affected California in 2017 had more than one cause. The state often depends on melting water from the Cascades and Sierra Nevada mountain ranges to provide water during the warmer months. Lately, the weather has been too warm for snow to settle on these mountains. In addition, while water can be pumped up from underground, this has been done too quickly in recent years, causing the supply to run out.

The United States Geological Survey has four major divisions, including hydrology, or the study of Earth's water. The other three divisions are biology, geography, and geology.

The 2017 drought, combined with the extremely hot California weather, helped contribute to some of the worst wildfires ever recorded in the state's history. The wildfires burned more than 280,000 acres (113,000 hectares) of land. The fire burned away plants, so when it began to rain, there were no plant roots or areas of loose soil to allow water to drain. The rain caused large chunks of land to break off hills, creating mudslides. Ultimately, these mudslides caused multiple deaths and millions of dollars in damage.

Experts working with the United States Geological Survey (USGS) have predicted that the area will be at risk of mudslides for years to come, due to the fires. Steps to help prevent future mudslides include digging basins to help control the flow of water. People in at-risk areas must also be ready to evacuate on short notice, if necessary.

The 2018 **California mudslides killed 21 people**.

Before the **California mudslides**, an **evacuation order** was given for **7,000** people.

The **California mudslides destroyed 59 homes**. They also damaged another 446.

Search and Rescue Workers

Search and rescue (SAR) workers respond to many kinds of disasters or events. They may help search for a single missing person or assist in locating dozens of people after a hurricane or flood. Different SAR jobs are based in various locations. No matter where SAR workers are stationed, it is important for them to know the area well. They need to be familiar with the geography, climate, and any hazards in the places they are searching.

United States Search and Rescue History

1915

The United States Coast Guard is formed. One of its main purposes is to rescue people at sea.

1983

The *SS Marine Electric* sinks off the coast of Virginia. The Coast Guard is only able to save 3 out of 34 crew members. As a result, the organization begins a rescue swimmer program the following year. Rescuers are trained to help people in the water.

1979

U.S. President Jimmy Carter signs an order creating the Federal Emergency Management Agency (FEMA). The agency's goal is to organize the federal government in preventing disasters and helping people when disasters do happen.

The tools and skills used by SAR workers depend on the areas in which they are operating. An SAR worker in the mountains might need to be a strong mountaineer. One on the coast could require diving skills and a familiarity with SCUBA gear. Other SAR workers may use search-and-rescue dogs to help find missing people. Many SAR workers must have first-aid training.

In the United States, there are several SAR organizations. The National Association For Search And Rescue (NASAR) was founded in 1972. It works across the country, in all environments. The United States Coast Guard exists to protect U.S. waters. On an average day, Coast Guard boats and aircraft perform more than 550 missions.

2005

The Coast Guard is one of the organizations that responds to Hurricane Katrina. SAR workers rescue more than 35,000 people from New Orleans.

2011

After Japan is struck by a powerful earthquake and tsunami, several nations, including the United States, send aid. Among these are SAR teams, sent to help the Japan Self-Defense Forces (JSDF). Emergency workers are able to rescue more than 15,000 people.

2017

Multiple organizations, including the U.S. Army, FEMA, and the Coast Guard, work to provide aid after Hurricane Maria strikes Puerto Rico. FEMA alone sends more than 10,000 federal staff members to Puerto Rico and the U.S. Virgin Islands to assist in SAR efforts.

Water-related Disasters around the World

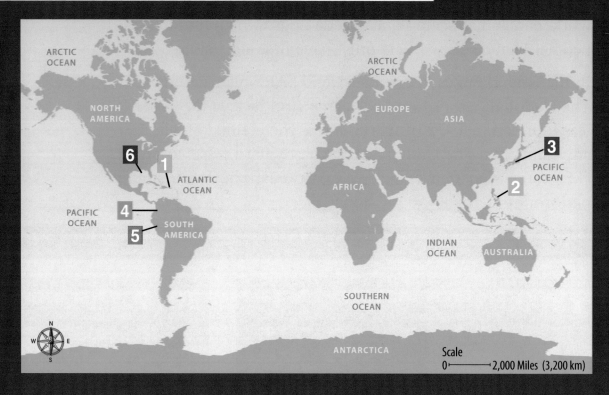

1 Hurricane Maria, Puerto Rico

Hurricane Maria made landfall in Puerto Rico in September 2017. At the time, it was a category 4 hurricane. Much of the territory's infrastructure was destroyed. Dozens of people were killed during the disaster. More than 80 percent of the island's electrical grid was taken offline.

2 Typhoon Haiyan, Philippines

Typhoon Haiyan, also known as Yolanda in the Philippines, was the strongest tropical storm recorded in 2013. It made landfall in the Philippines in early November. It had wind speeds of about 195 miles (313 km) per hour. By

the time the storm died down, more than 6,000 people had died and 3.9 million had to leave their homes.

3 2011 Japan Earthquake and Tsunami

One of the most powerful earthquakes ever recorded took place off the coast of Japan's main island, Honshu, in 2011. It created waves reaching heights of 33 feet (10 m) in Japan and 12 feet (3.6 m) in Hawai'i. The death toll of about 20,000 made this disaster one of the deadliest in Japan's history.

4 Armero Mudslide, Colombia

The volcano Nevado del Ruiz, also known as "the Sleeping Lion," erupted in 1985. The ice on the mountain's peak melted, causing a mudslide known as a lahar. This devastated the nearby town of Armero. More than 23,000 of Armero's 27,000 residents were killed by the mudslide.

5 Mount Huascaran Avalanche, Peru

In 1962, a large glacier on Mount Huascaran split, causing a massive avalanche of rock and ice. Although avalanches were common in the area, people usually had between 20 and 30 minutes to find safety once news of an avalanche spread. This disaster hit nearby towns after only 7 minutes. It led to approximately 4,000 deaths and the destruction of several towns.

6 Mississippi River Flood, United States

In April 1927, the Mississippi River flooded after months of heavy rain. Many levees surrounding the river collapsed over a period of weeks. After this, more than 23,000 square miles (60,000 sq. km) of land were flooded by waters that would remain in some places for more than two months.

Water Risk Management

People, organizations, and governments can take many different steps to prepare for or help prevent water-related disasters. Research online and in your library to find out how people have dealt with a water-related disaster near you.

WHAT HAPPENED?

Choose a water-related disaster that has taken place in your area. Note when it took place and what caused it. Was the disaster caused by nature or by humans? Could it happen again?

WHAT WAS THE EFFECT?

Find out how this disaster affected your area. How much damage did it cause? Were any people harmed by the disaster? What safety measures were in place to stop it? Did they work?

WHAT ACTIONS WERE TAKEN?

Research what happened after the disaster. How long did repairs take? Were any steps taken to make sure that this disaster could not happen again? Were any steps taken to prepare if it did happen again? Are there any steps that could have been taken, but were not?

Make a Tsunami

Instructions

Step 1: Remove any labels from the bottle. Fill it with 2 inches (5 centimeters) of gravel.

Step 2: Add 1 cup (237 milliliters) of water to the bottle. Screw on the cap.

Step 3: Slowly lay the bottle on its side. The gravel should form a hill at one side of the bottle.

Step 4: Lift up the top end of the bottle. Record your observations.

Step 5: Try the same experiment with half as much gravel. Then, try it again with twice as much. What differences and similarities are there? What does this tell you about how different kinds of coasts are affected by tsunamis?

Materials

Fish tank gravel

Measuring cup

Empty, clear 0.5-gallon (2-liter) plastic bottle

Water

Pen and paper

Quiz

Test your knowledge by answering these questions. All of the information can be found in the text you just read. The answers are provided below for easy reference.

1. What are the most dangerous kinds of floods?

2. Where did avalanches occur during World War I?

3. Are many people who work on SAR teams volunteers?

4. How many tornadoes can form in a hurricane?

5. Where did the largest recorded tsunami take place?

6. Where do avalanches occur?

7. Where do most tsunamis form?

8. What two disasters contributed to the 2018 California mudslides?

9. What does *tsunami* mean?

10. Which hurricane flooded New Orleans in 2005?

ANSWER KEY

1. Flash floods **2.** Italy **3.** Yes **4.** More than 140 **5.** Alaska **6.** At weak areas in snow **7.** The Pacific Ocean **8.** Wildfires and drought **9.** "Harbor wave" **10.** Hurricane Katrina

Key Words

coral reefs: lines made of the rocky material created by coral surrounding a coast

dams: barriers stopping water from moving down a river

debris: the remains of something that has been broken

drought: a dry period with little rain

equator: an imaginary line drawn around the middle of Earth

levees: steep slopes on the side of a river meant to stop it from flooding

organisms: living things, such as animals or plants

predicted: to have determined that something was going to happen based on evidence

seismic: relating to movement below Earth's surface

tectonic plates: large plates of land that make up Earth's surface

tsunamis: large waves caused by underwater earthquakes or other impacts

Index

LIGHTB◆X

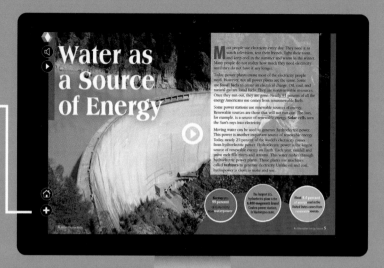

✚ SUPPLEMENTARY RESOURCES

Click on the plus icon ✚ found in the bottom left corner of each spread to open additional teacher resources.

- Download and print the book's quizzes and activities
- Access curriculum correlations
- Explore additional web applications that enhance the Lightbox experience

LIGHTBOX DIGITAL TITLES
Packed full of integrated media

VIDEOS

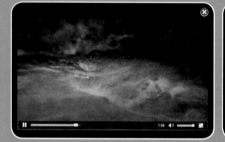

INTERACTIVE MAPS

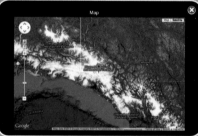

WEBLINKS

SLIDESHOWS

QUIZZES

OPTIMIZED FOR

✓ **TABLETS**
✓ **WHITEBOARDS**
✓ **COMPUTERS**
✓ **AND MUCH MORE!**

Published by Smartbook Media Inc.
350 5th Avenue, 59th Floor
New York, NY 10118
Website: www.openlightbox.com

Library of Congress Control Number:
2018944575

ISBN 978-1-5105-3889-4 (hardcover)
ISBN 978-1-5105-3890-0 (multi-user eBook)

Printed in Brainerd, Minnesota, United States
1 2 3 4 5 6 7 8 9 0 22 21 20 19 18

072018
120517

Project Coordinator John Willis
Art Director Terry Paulhus

Photo Credits
Every reasonable effort has been made to trace ownership and to obtain permission to reprint copyright material. The publisher would be pleased to have any errors or omissions brought to its attention so that they may be corrected in subsequent printings. The publisher acknowledges Alamy, Getty Images, iStock, Newscom, Shutterstock, and Wikimedia as its primary image suppliers for this title.